ESSENTIAL
SMALL
SPACES

TERENCE CONRAN

ESSENTIAL

SMALL

SPACES

THE BACK TO BASICS GUIDE TO HOME DESIGN, DECORATION & FURNISHING

conran
OCTOPUS

7/2/10

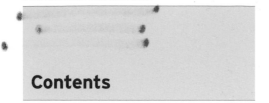

Contents

14

Planning & Design

INTRODUCTION

PLANNING & DESIGN

DECOR & FURNISHINGS

AREA BY AREA

Introduction

The premium price that space commands these days, particularly in dense urban areas, means that many of us are living in rather more circumscribed surroundings than we might prefer. Or it may be the case that our homes are more or less satisfactory, but we are feeling the pinch in certain key areas – perhaps the kitchen is too small or the bathroom is tiny.

Small-space living is generally perceived in negative terms because of the various challenges and difficulties it throws up. Where do you find space for your belongings? How do you accommodate your everyday routines and activities efficiently?

Whether living in a small space has been forced upon you out of economic necessity or is more of a positive choice, it is worth reminding yourself that there are significant advantages to the situation. Some people deliberately opt for a smaller home so that they can live in a better location, closer to where they work, for example, or within walking or cycling distance of shops and amenities. Others reach a stage in life where it is sensible to downsize to a home that requires less upkeep. Small spaces are undoubtedly easier to manage: clearing up and cleaning are less likely to present themselves as endless tasks that are no sooner completed than must begin all over again.

A small home is also far cheaper to run, notably in terms of energy bills and local rates and taxes. Similarly, when it comes to décor,

with less surface area to cover, you can afford better materials for flooring, walls and worktops, details which can give your home a real sense of character and quality.

To make the most of small spaces, a slightly different mindset is required. To begin with, you need to consider the space as a whole. Instead of thinking in terms of conventional rooms, each devoted to a separate function, it makes sense to arrange whatever space you have at your

LEFT: A MEZZANINE PROVIDES ENOUGH SPACE FOR A HIGH-LEVEL BED, WITH A COMPACT HOME OFFICE SLOTTED IN UNDERNEATH.

ABOVE: FITTED SOLUTIONS ARE OFTEN BEST FOR SMALL SPACES. IN THIS KITCHEN, NEAT, MINIMAL DETAILING KEEPS THE LOOK SEAMLESS AND UNCLUTTERED.

continued

Introduction

disposal in as flexible a way as possible, so that it can serve a number of related activities. Depending on circumstance and structural considerations, you may wish to include an eating area within your kitchen or opt for a fully open-plan arrangement where cooking, eating and relaxing all take place within the same multipurpose space. When it comes to small-space design a piecemeal approach rarely works.

It is fair to say that most successful small spaces include a significant proportion of fitted elements, particularly when it comes to storage. By building in as much as you can behind the scenes, you may lose a small amount of floor area, but the overall effect is much less visually intrusive than keeping things out on view.

Fitting out space with built-in fixtures calls for tight planning and careful construction, but the result often makes everyday tasks easier and more pleasant to perform. While a compact kitchen may be a one-person operation, if it is well organized it can be a joy to use, rather like operating an efficient machine. At their best, small spaces can perform every bit as well as larger ones, offering inclusive and flexible surroundings for everyday life.

Above all, small-space living forces you to be selective, both about what you own and what you do. You will not be able to house everything, so you will have to focus on what is truly important and only acquire what you use, love or need, which is by no means a bad thing.

ABOVE: A SEPARATE DINING ROOM IS A LUXURY WHEN SPACE IS TIGHT. THIS EATING AREA IS ARRANGED IN A CORNER OF A MULTIPURPOSE SPACE.

RIGHT: WORKING AREAS REQUIRE SOME SEPARATION FROM THE REST OF THE HOUSEHOLD. HERE, A WORK SURFACE OCCUPIES A RECESS IN FRONT OF A WINDOW.

INTRODUCTION

PLANNING & DESIGN

DECOR &

FURNISHINGS

AREA BY AREA

Assessing your needs

All homes, whatever their size, have to satisfy a number of basic needs. But how much space you give to different activities depends very much on your lifestyle and preferences. Spend some time thinking about your requirements to identify what is essential and what is less so.

- Do you like to entertain? Or are you at that stage of life where most of your socializing takes place away from home?
- Do friends or family regularly come to stay overnight or for longer periods?
- Do you work from home or bring work home on a regular basis? Does the type of work you do require a home office or studio? Is it largely computer-based or do you need somewhere to keep supplies and equipment?
- Do you like to cook or do you often eat out? Is your kitchen well-stocked or do you make do with the bare minimum in terms of food and equipment, buying only what you need each day?
- Is having a garden important to you?
- Do you shower rather than bathe? Could you manage without a bathtub?
- What type of possessions do you tend to accumulate?
- Think about the future. How long do you expect to remain in your present home and what changes in your lifestyle can you anticipate during that period?
- What is your budget?

ABOVE: SPIRAL STAIRS WITH OPEN FLIGHTS SAVE SPACE AND DO NOT BLOCK LIGHT UNNECESSARILY.

RIGHT: A LARGE PENDANT LIGHT SITED ABOVE A SMALL TABLE HELPS TO DEFINE THE EATING AREA IN A SLEEK CONTEMPORARY KITCHEN.

Spatial review

Careful planning is essential to make the most of the space at your disposal. First, get to know your home thoroughly. The most successful small spaces are often fitted in some way, with built-in cupboards, units and other features. This type of arrangement calls for a degree of precision – even a small amount of space can make the difference between a layout that works and one that is awkward.

- Put it down on paper. Measure each room or area in your home, note the dimensions on a sketch plan and work up scale plans on graph paper. For general living areas a scale of 1:50 is usually adequate. For kitchens and bathrooms, 1:20 will allow you to include more detail.
- Note down the size and dimensions of existing fittings and fixtures on your drawings. These may include fireplaces, power sockets, alcoves, windows and doors.
- Note basic orientation. Does the area get sun early in the day or later on?
- If you are planning extensive alterations, it is important to consult a surveyor to help you identify structural elements, such as load-bearing walls.
- As well as layout plans, elevations (plans of walls seen face on) can help you to decide where to put fixtures and fittings in kitchens and bathrooms.
- Cut out scale templates of furniture, fittings and appliances and move them around on your drawings to experiment with different layouts.

ABOVE: AN INTERNAL WINDOW ALLOWS LIGHT INTO A KITCHEN AND CREATES AN INTERNAL VISTA TO ENHANCE THE SENSE OF SPACE.

LEFT: A GENEROUS LANDING PROVIDES ENOUGH ROOM TO SET UP A HOME OFFICE. THINK LATERALLY ABOUT HOW YOU USE THE SPACE AT YOUR DISPOSAL.

Clearing out clutter

Many of the problems people experience with small spaces are to do with not having enough places to put things. Whether you are living in a small flat or apartment until you can afford something bigger or downsizing to a smaller home after the family has flown the nest, take the time to have a thorough clear-out. Keep only what you really need and love.

- In certain cases, you may find that your present circumstances make an entire category of possessions redundant. If you no longer have a garden, for example, or your garden is small and requires only minimal maintenance, you probably will not need much in the way of gardening equipment.
- Get rid of anything that is broken, damaged beyond repair, past its sell-by-date or in any sense unusable. This applies as much to basic supplies as it does to equipment and books.
- Get rid of any possessions that you do not like. Be ruthless with yourself – guilt often stands in the way of letting things go.
- Get rid of things that you do not use anymore, such as sports or leisure equipment relating to an activity that you no longer pursue.
- Most people only wear about 20 per cent of the clothes that they own. Pare down your wardrobe to the items of clothing that you actually wear on a regular basis.
- Get rid of duplicate items.
- Review your archives and get rid of any documents, old bills and instruction manuals that are no longer relevant.

ABOVE: STORAGE IS A CRITICAL ISSUE WHEN YOUR HOME IS SMALL. THIS RECLAIMED GLASS-FRONTED WOODEN CABINET HOUSES CROCKERY AND TABLEWARE.

RIGHT: SHELVING BUILT INTO AN ALCOVE READS AS PART OF THE ARCHITECTURAL DETAILING OF THE ROOM.

Servicing

When you are living in a small space, the basic infrastructure of your home – how power, water and heat is delivered – should be as discreet and as flexible as possible. Before you undertake any major improvements, think about whether making changes to servicing might improve your options for layout or make existing conditions more workable.

Heating

- Underfloor heating is the most discreet kind. Systems that rely on heated water require more depth of subfloor than electric versions. Underfloor heating works best with solid, massive flooring materials, such as stone and concrete, which release heat slowly. Certain types of floor covering, such as wood laminate, are not suitable for use with underfloor heating.
- There are a number of space-saving radiators on the market, including slim-line versions, low-level radiators that hug the base of the wall, and vertical designs, many of which have a contemporary sculptural appeal.

Power

- A choice of power points adds flexibility to a layout. Ensure that you have enough points for your needs to prevent overloaded sockets and cables trailing over the floor.
- Plan a lighting scheme in tandem with other spatial improvements. Fixed lighting can be disruptive to install once you have decorated.

Water & drainage

Of all forms of servicing, water and drainage are the most complicated, expensive and disruptive to change. Unless you have very pressing reasons for making an alteration, you will need to plan fitted kitchens and bathrooms around existing arrangements.

ABOVE: BATHROOMS SHOULD BE PLANNED AROUND EXISTING SERVICING. THIS FULLY FITTED BATHROOM HAS BEEN CONCEIVED AS A WHOLE TO CREATE A BRIGHT, STREAMLINED SPACE.

LEFT: LIGHTING CONCEALED BEHIND A MARGIN OF LOWERED CEILING WASHES THE TOP OF THE ROOM WITH LIGHT TO ENHANCE THE OVERHEAD SPACE.

Open layouts

Layouts with as few internal divisions as possible are naturally space-enhancing. Taking down a wall will not give you much additional floor area, but it will allow light to spill through and will also introduce internal vistas, both of which make the limitations of a small space less noticeable. However, it is important to balance open areas with more private, enclosed places where you can retreat for some peace and quiet.

- Knocking two rooms together by removing a wall will create a feeling of spaciousness. The expense and disruption of the work will depend on whether the wall is structural. If it is, you will need to add a steel joist or some other compensating element to bear the load previously supported by the wall.
- A hallway can be absorbed into a living area by removing the wall that divides the two spaces.
- Opening up the stairs by removing the wall that encloses them can create enough space for a desk or extra storage. You may need to check that such an alteration is permissible under fire regulations.
- Removing portions of partition walls will provide views through the space and spread natural light around. A narrow vertical or horizontal opening can provide tantalizing glimpses from area to area. This is often a good strategy where bathrooms or kitchens are fully internal.
- Be aware that you will need an architect or a structural engineer to approve your plans for structural change.

ABOVE: A MEZZANINE LEVEL PROVIDES A SLEEPING AREA IN A DOUBLE-HEIGHT SPACE. MEZZANINES SHOULD BE POSITIONED WHERE THEY WILL NOT BLOCK LIGHT AND VIEWS.

RIGHT: A HALF-HEIGHT, HALF-WIDTH PARTITION SEPARATES A FITTED KITCHEN FROM AN EATING AREA.

Continued

Open layouts

Increasing natural light

The quality of natural light makes an enormous difference to how spacious a room feels. Changing existing windows or putting in new openings can have a dramatic effect on the way you experience your home. In many cases, such alterations involve structural work.

■ Removing the portion of wall underneath an existing window sill to lengthen the window and create a door is straightforward to carry out and does not have structural implications. As well as increasing levels of natural light, you can also improve access to outdoor areas.

■ You can widen an existing window either to create a picture window from two adjacent sashes, or to install French windows or sliding glazed panels to improve access to a garden or balcony. Here you will need to install a joist or some other structural member across the new opening to compensate for the loss of the load-bearing wall.

■ Creating a completely new opening is another way to bring in light. Think about where best to site a new window, with respect to orientation and views. Making a new window in an external wall is structural work and you will need to install a beam over the new opening.

■ Rooflights, skylights and other forms of high-level window draw light down into a space. How much light a window admits to the interior depends on how much sky it reveals: the higher the window, the brighter the light.

ABOVE: AN INTERNAL KITCHEN BORROWS LIGHT FROM WINDOWS TO THE FRONT AND SIDE.

LEFT: A GLAZED PANEL SCREENING A STAIRCASE ALLOWS NATURAL LIGHT TO SPILL DOWN FROM ABOVE.

Continued

Open layouts

Volume

Rooms with high ceilings, or whose 'volume' is greater, naturally feel more uplifting. Creating variations in volume may entail the loss of some space, but the expansive effect can be worth it.

- Cutting away a portion of an upper floor to create a double-height space introduces a sense of drama.
- Raising a portion of floor up a few steps to create a platform helps to distinguish between different activities within an open-plan layout.
- If you are converting a loft that is double-height or has very high ceilings, stopping partitions short of the ceiling allows the volume of the space to be read as a whole.

Minimizing detail

Architectural details, such as cornices, skirting boards and picture rails, break up the plane of a wall and can contribute to a sense of enclosure.

- One way of minmizing architectural elements is to paint all such features, including doors and woodwork, the same colour as the walls.
- If you are remodelling, you may wish to remove unnecessary details, such as dados and picture rails, altogether.
- In the absence of skirting boards you can stop the plasterwork short of the floor, a technique known as shadow-gapping. The lower portion of the plasterwork is supported by a profiled metal strip and the gap gives a crisp edge.

ABOVE: THIS STORAGE CABINET IS ATTACHED TO THE WALL LEAVING THE FLOOR VISIBLE UNDERNEATH FOR A MORE SPACIOUS EFFECT.

RIGHT: HERE, WALLS AND SHELVING ARE PAINTED THE SAME COLOUR SO THAT THE SPACE READS AS A WHOLE. SIMPLE DETAILING IS LESS INTRUSIVE.

Mezzanines

In areas where ceilings are above standard height, creating a mezzanine or even a high-level platform can win you additional floor area. Adding a mezzanine, where the load of the floor is carried by existing walls, is structural work and you will need professional help. A platform can be constructed more simply by making use of the top of a freestanding structure or building up from the floor.

- Siting is important. It is generally best to add a mezzanine or platform where it will not block light and views.
- Size is also critical. The mezzanine should not be so extensive that it begins to affect the spatial quality of the level below.
- A platform used for sleeping does not require full head height. It can also be relatively narrow, provided there is enough space for a bed and enough margin for access.
- Decide whether or not you want to screen the mezzanine with some form of balustrading, such a glazed panels.
- Think about how you are going to access the new level. Space-saving stairs include paddle steps and spiral stairs.
- The area under a mezzanine or platform can be fitted out in a number of ways. Kitchens, bathrooms, work spaces and built-in storage can be slotted in underneath.

ABOVE: A SIMPLE RAISED PLATFORMS CAN BE BUILT UP FROM THE FLOOR. THIS SLEEPING PLATFORM HAS CLOTHES STORAGE FITTED UNDERNEATH.

LEFT: A MEZZANINE IS A GOOD PLACE FOR ACTIVITIES THAT REQUIRE SOME PRIVACY, SUCH AS SLEEPING OR WORKING. THIS HIGH-LEVEL OFFICE BENEFITS FROM AN ABUNDANCE OF NATURAL LIGHT.

Building in flexibility

Flexibility is increasingly what we demand of our homes today. When space is limited, many areas will inevitably function as multipurpose zones, which makes it even more important to build in a degree of adaptability. This can be achieved in a number of ways: by altering internal doors, using screens and partitions, simplifying routes, or by fitting out spaces with elements that pull down, pull out or fold away.

Changes to doors
- A standard door defines a particular area as a separate room. If you extend the doorway right up to the ceiling, the floor and ceiling planes are unobstructed, which enhances the sense of space.
- Sliding doors or panels are more space-saving than those that open outwards or inwards.
- Glazed or semi-transparent internal doors spread light around.

Screens & partitions
- Movable screens and partitions allow you to keep your options open. Sliding or folding doors can be used to partition a shared children's bedroom during the night, for example, and left open during the day.
- Room dividers in the form of freestanding modular units can effectively separate different activities within an open-plan layout.
- Solid partitions that are half-width or half-height preserve the unity of the space while providing a degree of separation.
- Mirrors will give the effect of doubling your space.

ABOVE: AN OPEN MODULAR ROOM DIVIDER DOUBLES UP AS A PLACE FOR STORAGE AND DISPLAY.

RIGHT: TALL SLIDING DOORS SEPARATE A KITCHEN FROM A DINING ROOM.

Continued

Building in flexibility

Simplifying routes

Think about the way you move about your home via the connecting spaces of stairs, halls and landings. If these are cramped or awkward, it can reinforce the feeling that your home is too small to be comfortable.

- Make a sketch plan of the layout of your home and mark on the main routes from place to place. Where are the bottlenecks? Where does clutter tend to build up? If you keep bicycles in a hall, for example, an overhead racking system might improve accessibility.
- If a room or area has two access doors, one entrance will probably be favoured over the other. Blocking up the redundant doorway can give you more useful wall area to either side of the partition.
- Changing a door so that it opens outwards rather than inwards, or vice versa, can make a significant difference.

Fitted elements

Articulated, fitted elements, such as panels, flaps and surfaces that pull out, pull down or fold away, build an element of flexibility into the fabric of a space. Housed within working walls of storage, fold-down beds and pull-out tables or desks can be hidden away behind flush panels when not in use. However, they must be designed, detailed and constructed so that they are easy to operate.

LEFT: A LARGE SLIDING PANEL OF FROSTED GLASS SCREENS KITCHEN ACTIVITY WITHOUT BLOCKING LIGHT.

ABOVE: CONCERTINA DOORS THAT FOLD BACK AGAINST THEMSELVES MAKE FLEXIBLE PARTITIONING.

Using redundant space

Even in the smallest homes, it is possible to identify space that is under used. In older properties, for example, circulation areas may be disproportionately generous, which provides an opportunity to adapt them for other functions.

Stairs, halls & landings

- If your bathroom is small and adjacent to a relatively generous landing, moving the partition wall forwards a little will improve your options for bathroom layout without compromising main traffic routes.
- Spacious landings can make convenient storage areas. You can build in cupboards or shelves, or use freestanding pieces of furniture such as chests and armoires.
- An alternative is to set up a working area or compact home office on a landing, a location that provides sufficient separation from the rest of the household. Installing a rooflight or skylight over the landing will improve natural light and generate a feeling of expansiveness.
- If your hallway is wide enough, consider devoting an entire wall to built-in storage, either shelving or concealed cupboards.
- The area below the stairs is another useful between-space. You can make a simple cupboard by shelving the recess and fitting doors to the front. Built-in stepped cupboards or pull-out racks exploit every bit of space. Alternatively, you can fit out the area with shelving and a worksurface to create a compact home office.

ABOVE: A CUSTOM-DESIGNED STAIRCASE IS FITTED OUT WITH INTEGRATED STORAGE CONCEALED BEHIND VENEERED PANELS.

RIGHT: A SIMILAR APPROACH SHOWS AN UNDER-STAIRS SPACE COMPARTMENTALIZED WITH CUBBYHOLES.

Continued

Using redundant space

Attics

Converting an attic into a habitable room is a relatively straightforward way of substantially increasing your floor area.

- Head height is a key consideration. At least half the converted space should have a head height of 2.3m (7½ft).
- You will need to install at least one window, preferably one that opens. Options include rooflights and skylights that sit flush with the plane of the roof or dormers that project out.
- If you will be using the space on a daily basis, you will require a permanent fixed stair of some kind.
- Structural work includes doubling up floor joists to strengthen them and doubling up roof rafters to either side of new openings.

- A number of rules apply regarding fire regulations and means of access. You may also require planning permission, particularly if you will be altering the external appearance of your house from the street.

Basements

Basement conversions are increasingly popular, due to new techniques for controlling damp. However, they are very expensive and disruptive to carry out, and much depends on existing ground conditions. If you have a full or semi-basement it is less problematic to devote the entire area to storage, provided it is not damp or at risk of flooding. It is wise to pack items away in waterproof, rigid, lidded containers. Make sure that you label them and keep a record of what you have stored there.

LEFT: A SECURE MEANS OF ACCESS IS NECESSARY IF YOU ARE GOING TO USE A CONVERTED ATTIC OR A PLATFORM LEVEL ON A REGULAR BASIS.

ABOVE: ALMOST ALL ATTICS CAN BE CONVERTED, EVEN THOSE WITH PREFORMED ROOF TRUSSES. THIS ONE HAS BEEN MADE INTO AN ELEGANT PLACE TO RELAX.

Compact stairs

You can gain extra floor area if you replace a conventional staircase, which takes up a lot of room with turns and landings, with a space-saving stair. These designs are ideal for providing access to converted attics or mezzanine levels, where you want to avoide losing floor area on the level below. Whichever you choose, it must be adequate for the job it has to do and should conform to building regulations and codes.

Types of compact stair

- Spiral stairs turn around a central support and come in a wide range of designs and materials. Some have universal platforms that can be adapted to square or circular stairwells. Cast-iron period examples are very heavy and you will need to establish that the floor can bear the weight.
- Paddle steps have offset treads which makes them much narrower than conventional designs. These can be vertical or canted.
- Open-tread stairs can enhance a feeling of space because they do not block light or views. At their most minimal, they can be cantilevered from the wall.
- Attic ladders are available in a wide range of formats and materials. A ladder in regular use must be robust.
- Bespoke stair design can result in ingenious storage solutions, such as treads that double up as cubbyholes or drawers for stowing away various items.

ABOVE: PADDLE OR MONK'S STEPS ARE MUCH NARROWER THAN CONVENTIONAL STAIRS BECAUSE THE TREADS ARE OFF-SET.

RIGHT: SPIRAL STAIRS, LIKE THESE METAL ONES, ARE A POPULAR SPACE-SAVING OPTION. YOU NEED TO CHECK THAT THE FLOOR CAN BEAR THE WEIGHT.

Storage

Small-space living presents particular challenges when it comes to storage. It is best to consider what your storage needs are overall and think about ways of accommodating them throughout your entire home, rather than react retrospectively or in a piecemeal fashion.

The first step is to determine levels of accessibility. The things you use on a daily basis need to be kept in close proximity to the place where you will be using them: bath products next to the bath or shower, basic kitchen equipment next to the main preparation area. Alternatively, belongings that see rare or seasonal use should be stored in out-of-the way locations. The remainder of your belongings will require logical systems of organization and should be easy to access.

The best storage solutions for small spaces tend to be fitted, which demands careful planning. Although building in fitted storage does entail the loss of some floor area, the result will be much less visually intrusive, particularly if cupboards are concealed behind flush panels. Freestanding storage furniture, on the other hand, unless tucked into recesses or alcoves, tends to result in awkward margins of unusable floor space to either side, and is much more dominant in appearance.

LEFT: SHELVING PROVIDES CONVENIENT STORAGE FOR MANY TYPES OF POSSESSIONS. SHELF DEPTH AND HEIGHT CAN BE MODIFIED TO SUIT PARTICULAR ITEMS.

ABOVE: THE COMPACT NATURE OF MODERN MEDIA SYSTEMS MAKES IT EASY TO CONCEAL THEM BEHIND PANELS OR WITHIN FITTED CUPBOARDS.

Continued

Storage

Planning fitted storage

Whether you are buying fitted storage off the peg or commissioning a bespoke storage system, it is useful to sketch out various options on paper first. These initial thoughts can form the basis of a brief for a builder or can be worked up in more detail in consultation with an in-house design service from your retailer.

- Make scale drawings of the areas in which you plan to build in storage so that you can determine exactly how much space you have to play with and how best to accommodate fixed points in the layout, such as the position of bathroom and kitchen servicing.
- Consult catalogues and brochures to get an idea of the common dimensions of fitted wall and base units, wardrobes and cupboards.
- Make a rough estimate of the amount you need to store and do not forget to allow a margin for future acquisitions.
- Pay attention to scale and proportion so that the fitted storage blends in with the existing architectural character. Low-level cupboards or shelving running around the perimeter of a room suit contemporary interiors where ceilings are lower and which have more of a horizontal emphasis. In older properties, alcoves to either side of the chimneybreast are natural places for fitted storage.
- If at all possible, adopt a whole-hearted approach: for example, shelve an entire wall from floor to ceiling or devote a whole wall to fitted cupboards.

ABOVE: WHATEVER YOU KEEP ON VIEW SHOULD EITHER CONTRIBUTE VISUAL INTEREST OR BE IN REGULAR USE.

RIGHT: FITTED CUPBOARDS WITH CHAMFERED PULLS OR PRESS-CATCHES ARE CLEAN-LINED AND DISCREET. UNINTERRUPTED PLANES ENHANCE SPACE.

Continued

Storage

Shelving

- Shelving should suit the height and depth of the items you are storing. Look out for storage units that feature adjustable shelves so that you can customize the interiors of cupboards according to your requirements. Many commercially available shelving systems designed for books or other objects are also adjustable, which allows you to experiment with spacing.
- Depth is a critical factor. Narrow shelves are good for storing small items, such as herbs and spices, medicines and remedies, and also for storing fragile items, such as glassware.

Customizing fitted storage

- Retailers and storage specialists produce a wide range of accessories, such as drawer dividers and racks, to ensure that fitted units can be used to their fullest extent. If you are on a tight budget, you can improvise with boxes, jars, baskets and other containers.
- You can give existing fitted storage a make-over by replacing doors and drawer fronts and upgrading catches and handles. Some companies specialize in replacement doors for standard kitchen and bathroom units; otherwise you can commission a carpenter to make new doors for you.

ABOVE: DEVOTING AN ENTIRE WALL TO FITTED STORAGE WORKS BEST. HERE, RANDOM CUPBOARD DOORS PICKED OUT IN BOLD COLOURS CREATES A GRAPHIC FEATURE.

LEFT: ONE WALL OF A BROAD HALLWAY HAS BEEN LINED WITH RECESSES AND DRAWERS TO HOUSE A WARDROBE.

INTRODUCTION
PLANNING & DESIGN
DECOR & FURNISHINGS
AREA BY AREA

Basic considerations

Making appropriate décor and furnishing choices will not overcome the physical limitations of a small space, but they can help to enhance a feeling of openness and expansion.

- Unity is the key to successful small space decorating and furnishing. It is important to think about your home as a whole rather than approaching each area individually.
- In a small space abrupt changes of décor can undermine spatial quality, particularly where there are views from one area to another. While you do not have to treat every room the same, one or two consistent themes, such as a colour scheme or a particular type of flooring, will help to tie everything together.
- Create a mood board to help you visualize your proposed interior scheme. Assemble samples and swatches of materials so that you can try out different combinations. Catalogue photography and showroom displays can be misleading and there is no substitute for the real thing. Collect as many samples as you can and view them under normal light conditions at home to judge their impact. You do not want to wait until the floor is laid to discover that that tiles look much darker *in situ* than they did in the shop.

ABOVE: WALLS ARE PAINTED A SOFT STONE COLOUR AND FLOORING IS CARPETED THROUGHOUT TO CREATE A SENSE OF UNITY.

RIGHT: INTENSE COLOUR CAN BE USED SPARINGLY AS AN ACCENT OR CONTAINED WITHIN A SEPARATE AREA, SUCH AS A BATHROOM.

Lighting

Good lighting is always important and in small spaces it is crucial. A well-thought-out lighting scheme can make cramped surroundings appear much more spacious and hospitable. Many people treat lighting as an afterthought or pay more attention to the style of fittings and lamps than they do to the quality of light they emit. Instead, lighting should be planned very early on in tandem with other spatial improvements. To experiment with lighting arrangements, equip yourself with a number of basic lights, such as clip-on spots or small table lamps, then direct light at different parts of a room and try out different levels and positions. Most areas in the home require a combination of at least two different types of lighting.

- Gentle background or ambient light can be supplied by uplighters, downlighters, wall-washers, side lights and track lights, as well as by floor and table lamps. The light source should be diffused in some way or concealed to avoid glare.
- Directional or task light, supplied by spotlights, adjustable track fittings and desk lamps, provides a boost of illumination for working areas or displays.
- Architectural lighting, where strip lights or single spotlights are concealed behind baffles, underneath wall-hung units or positioned at low level underneath built-in fixtures and fittings, highlight architectural detail and reduce the apparent bulk of large features.

LEFT: LIGHTING RECESSED IN THE BASE OF A WALL CREATES AN ILLUMINATED PATHWAY THAT LEADS THE EYE UPWARDS TO THE TOP OF THE STAIRWAY.

ABOVE: A NICHE IS LIT BY CONCEALED DOWNLIGHTS THAT EMPHASIZE THE DECORATIVE OBJECTS ON DISPLAY AS WELL AS ILLUMINATING THE ROOM.

Continued

Lighting

ABOVE: A LIGHTWELL BRINGS DAYLIGHT DOWN INTO A
BASEMENT WHICH HAS BEEN EXCAVATED UNDERNEATH
AN EXISTING PROPERTY.

RIGHT: LIGHT FLOODS INTO A ROOM THROUGH A GLAZED
WALL. INCREASING THE SIZE OF EXISTING OPENINGS
CAN IMPROVE THE QUALITY OF NATURAL LIGHT AND
MAKE A SPACE SEEM BIGGER.

Lighting small spaces

- Always switch lights on before you purchase them to gauge their effect. All fixed forms of lighting should be installed by a qualified professional, preferably before final decoration takes place to minimize disruption.
- Avoid central or overhead lights wherever possible. A single overhead light causes glare, which is tiring and depressing, and casts shadows into corners, which makes rooms feel smaller.
- Increase the number of light sources. Even in a smallish living room, you will need four to five different light sources. Varying their positions and heights to create overlapping pools of light and shade will lead the eye from place to place.
- Restrict the use of downlights to areas where the layout is fixed, such as kitchens and bathrooms. In living areas, they can limit your options for furniture arrangement.
- Bounce light off the reflective planes of walls and ceilings to create a diffused glow. Targeting light at the ceiling makes a room seem higher; targeting light at the walls makes the room feel bigger. This strategy is most effective when walls and ceilings are light in tone.
- Lighting concealed underneath fitted units minimizes their bulk. Similarly, floor-level lights accentuate a sense of progression from area to area.
- Wall wash lighting is very economical to install and produces a very restful ambiance.
- Fit dimmer switches to vary the mood in multipurpose areas.

Decorative strategies

The basic decorative palette of colour, pattern and texture is expressed in the surfaces and finishes we choose for our homes: wall and window treatments, floor coverings and worktops. The aim of small space decoration is to enhance the effect of natural and artificial light and create a sense of unity and spaciousness.

Using colour

- For background colours, it is usually best to opt for shades that reflect light or come from the cooler end of the spectrum, which means white, colours that contain a lot of white, and various shades of blue. Cool colours are 'distancing', which means that surfaces and finishes painted or decorated in these shades will tend to look farther away, creating a naturally expansive effect.
- Consider orientation: if a room faces north and east, cool colours can be a little too chilly. Warm off-whites and creams are better.
- Pale and neutral may be a fail-safe strategy but can be bland and boring. For drama, opt for all-white decoration, which packs a more powerful punch. Choose your whites carefully: good quality white paint, for example, costs more, but has an unmistakeable sophistication and ages well.

LEFT: PALE COLOURS ARE NATURALLY SPACE-ENHANCING AND RESTFUL, IDEAL FOR MAKING THE MOST OF AVAILABLE DAYLIGHT.

ABOVE: TEXTURAL CONTRAST IS AN IMPORTANT ELEMENT WHERE DECORATIVE SCHEMES ARE OTHERWISE RESTRAINED.

Continued

Decorative strategies

Textural contrast

In confined spaces where strong colour and busy patterns can be overwhelming, texture supplies an extra dimension that adds depth and character. You can achieve interesting textural contrasts by juxtaposing reflective materials with patterning, such as wood grain or tilework, or tactile soft furnishings.

- In most cases, natural materials are preferable to synthetic ones because they age well and acquire an attractive patina over time. There is also the issue of comfort. Upholstery, cushion and pillow covers, and bed and bath linen in natural fibres feel better next to the skin than artificial fibres.
- Highly reflective materials, such as glass, stainless steel, mirror, along with lacquered and polished finishes, make the most of available light.
- Textural contrast is particularly effective underfoot. If you restrict your choice of flooring materials to those that are pale or neutral in tone, you can still ring the changes by varying the material. Pale wood flooring in a living area can give way to stone tiles of a similar tone in a kitchen without undermining any sense of coherence.
- One advantage of small space decorating is that you may find you can afford to use materials of a better quality because there is less surface area to cover.

ABOVE: A WOOD FLOOR JUXTAPOSED WITH REFLECTIVE KITCHEN SURFACES ADDS CHARACTER AND INTEREST.

RIGHT: THESE TILES MAKE A STRONG GRAPHIC STATEMENT. DENSE PATTERN, LIKE STRONG COLOUR, IS OFTEN BEST RESTRICTED TO SELF-CONTAINED AREAS.

Continued

Decorative strategies

Bold statements

You need not forego strong colour and bold patterning just because your home is on the small side, but such attention-seeking elements do require careful handling. It is essential to provide plenty of breathing space so the effect is not too overwhelming.

- Use bright colour and strong pattern as accents. Cushions, throws and upholstery in vivid hues and eye-catching designs provide a jolt of interest when backgrounds are unassuming; most are economical to change if you get tired of them. A siren-red fridge or navy blue range can also make a strong statement in an otherwise neutral kitchen.
- Using a slightly larger dose of colour or pattern as a focal point is another strategy. One wall picked out in a strong colour or papered in a striking print can provide a visual anchor for furniture arrangement in an open-plan space.
- Another option is to restrict colour or pattern to a self-contained area. The use of strong colour can be surprisingly effective in hallways and stairs, where it can serve as a vivid thread tying different spaces together. Shades that might be too dominating for living areas add a touch of vitality to brief journeys around the home. The same is true of bathrooms and cloakrooms, where you do not spend vast amounts of time.

ABOVE: WITH THE PRINCIPAL BACKGROUND COLOURS WHITE OR NEUTRAL, COLOUR CAN BE INTRODUCED IN THE FORM OF BRIGHT ACCENTS.

LEFT: WALLS PAINTED IN A SOFT SHADE OF BLUE PROVIDE A GENTLE WASH OF COLOUR IN A BATHROOM TUCKED UNDER THE EAVES.

Furniture & arrangement

Less is definitely more when it comes to furnishing a small space. Freestanding pieces devour floor area and quickly make a room look cluttered. In this context, less also means simplicity – clean lines and a lack of fussy detail work best. A clear floor and unobstructed sightlines also help to give a sense of space.

Large pieces of furniture

Every home, no matter how cramped, will require at least a couple of large pieces of furniture: a double bed, a sofa and possibly a dining or work table. When you are choosing a large item of furniture, you need to make sure that it will actually fit into the space you have allotted for it, as well as through the front door, and possibly around a couple of stair returns. Scale drawings can be helpful to determine whether or not this will be possible. Some designs have legs that can be unscrewed or other detachable parts to make them easier to manoeuvre around tight corners.

Do not be tempted to opt for very small-scale pieces that might not deliver the basic comfort and practicality that you need. Smaller is not always the answer. Under-scaled furniture can give your home a certain meanness and the look of a doll's house.

ABOVE: PLACE LARGE PIECES OF FURNITURE, SUCH AS SOFAS, IN RECESSES OR BACK AGAINST THE WALLS TO KEEP FLOOR AREA CLEAR.

RIGHT: LOW MODULAR SEATING UPHOLSTERED IN WHITE IS A GOOD CHOICE FOR SMALL LIVING AREAS. BRIGHT CUSHIONS PROVIDE COLOUR ACCENTS.

Continued

Furniture & arrangement

Reducing the impact

- Arrange furniture to take advantage of recesses and alcoves to keep as much of the floor area clear as possible.
- Keep it simple. A pair of matching sofas may provide all the seating you need and will look neater than an assortment of armchairs and occasional chairs of different sizes and types.
- Furniture that has a strong horizontal emphasis, such as sofas with low backs, modular seating and floor-level beds, will make an area seem bigger and are also ideal for rooms with low ceilings, such as attic conversions. High-backed furniture, by contrast, interrupts sightlines.
- Choose simple, discreet designs, rather than traditional pieces. A divan bed, for example, does not proclaim its function, which means that it can be used as additional seating in the daytime should circumstances require it.
- See-through designs, such as glass tables, Perspex chairs, and seating with wire or mesh frameworks, are less dominant. Lightweight garden furniture can also work well.
- Keep upholstery plain and understated. Large pieces upholstered in white or neutral shades have less visual impact than those with an eye-catching pattern. If you are worried about upkeep, choose washable loose covers.
- Be careful with lighting. Do not draw attention to large pieces of furniture by lighting them directly. Place lights in the spaces between furniture or target lighting so that it is reflected from the walls and ceiling. Under-lighting beds, built-in storage and other bulky features makes them appear to float over the floor.

ABOVE: TRANSPARENT FURNITURE, SUCH AS A GLASS-TOPPED TABLE, HERE ACCOMPANIED BY CLEAR PLASTIC CHAIRS, IS LESS DOMINANT.

LEFT: LARGE FLOOR-LEVEL CUSHIONS MAKE UNOBTRUSIVE ADDITIONAL SEATING. A PALE RUG DEFINES A CONVERSATION AREA AND PROVIDES COMFORT UNDERFOOT.

Continued

Furniture & arrangement

Multipurpose & transformable furniture

Pieces of furniture that serve more than one purpose or ones that can be easily stowed away are ideal solutions where space is tight.

Tables

- Space-saving tables include simple surfaces or panels that fold-down from the wall. These require secure anchorage. Some kitchen manufacturers include such features within their ranges; otherwise you can commission a design from a carpenter or builder.
- Gate-leg, drop-leaf and extending tables with leaves allow you to accommodate more people for a special occasion.
- Occasional tables that stack, nest or fold away are easy to store when not in use.

Beds

- Fold-down beds offer real flexibility when it comes to multipurpose spaces. Modern designs are comfortable and well-engineered. There is a huge range of beds on the market: single, double and master sizes, fold-down bunk beds, desk-to-bed conversions and wall beds that form part of fitted storage. Most companies that supply folding beds provide an installation service.
- Sofa beds are a popular way of providing an extra bed for overnight guests. Invest in the best you can afford: cheap sofa beds tend not to provide enough support in either format.
- Futons are another good option as they can be rolled up to provide seating during the day.

Seating

- Folding chairs, which can be easily stored, enable you to accommodate guests from time to time without cluttering up your living space on a daily basis. These come in a wide range of designs and materials.
- Stacking stools and chairs can double up as additional seating and stools can act as side tables.

ABOVE: ELEGANT OCCASIONAL TABLES SLOT NEATLY TOGETHER WHEN NOT IN USE.

RIGHT: LOW BENCHES HOUSE A COLLECTION OF OLD VINYL RECORDS, WHILE ADDITIONAL SEATING IS PROVIDED BY LOW STOOLS.

Detail

In a small space, any form of clutter rapidly undermines any feeling of spaciousness. On the other hand, empty rooms can be rather sterile and soulless. While you have to be more selective about what you include, it is important to provide the eye with something to gaze upon and linger over. There are two basic kinds of detail: those that are functional and those that contribute aesthetic pleasure.

Working details

These include doorknobs, power points, handrails, switches and a host of other small-scale elements designed to perform a particular function. There are a number of ways in which such details can be treated in a small space.

- If you are keen on a seamless look, many working details can be suppressed or completely omitted. Concealed chamfered finger-pulls or press-catches obviate the need for door and drawer handles. Clear plastic or glass switch plates are visually discreet.
- Be consistent. In a small space, details are much more noticeable. It is a good idea to use the same type and material throughout your home – if you have brushed-metal socket plates in the kitchen, for example, you should install the same elsewhere.
- Invest in quality. An advantage of small-space living is that you will need fewer working details and therefore can afford to invest in better-quality designs.

ABOVE: OVER-SCALED D-HANDLES, WHICH EMPHASIZE THE VERTICAL PLANE, HAVE BEEN FITTED TO SLIDING PANELS THAT PARTITION A MULTIPURPOSE SPACE.

LEFT: GOOD-QUALITY STAINLESS STEEL HANDLES LEND A TOUCH OF CLASS TO A FITTED KITCHEN.

Display

Whatever you keep out on view in a small space should earn its keep in some way, either because it provides visual pleasure or is in regular use.

- Working displays can provide a point of interest in sleek contemporary interiors. Kitchen utensils, pencil jars, and bathroom accessories, such as sponges and brushes, are all items that can be left out on view if artfully grouped.
- Natural places for decorative displays, aside from walls, include mantelpieces, niches, tabletops, shelving and storage units.
- Areas of transition, such as hallways and landings, can be good places for display.
- Allow plenty of breathing space so that what you put on view can be fully appreciated.
- Group items together that have some common denominator – colour, form or type – and arrange them in one location so that the collection reads as a whole.
- Vary what you put out on view from time to time. Propping pictures rather than hanging them makes it easy to swap things round.
- Accent lighting of some form or another gives displays added interest. You can pick out an object in a narrow beam of light, use side light to accentuate form and texture, or back light to enhance an object's material quality, such as the transparency of glass, for example.

ABOVE: A FRAMELESS GLASS PANEL CREATES AN ELEGANTLY DETAILED MAGAZINE RACK.

RIGHT: FOR A SEAMLESS LOOK, FITTED STORAGE IS CONCEALED BEHIND PLAIN WHITE PANELS WITH PRESS-CATCHES. UNDERLIGHTING REDUCES VISUAL BULK.

INTRODUCTION
PLANNING & DESIGN
DECOR & FURNISHINGS
AREA BY AREA

Multipurpose areas

When space is tight, many areas in the home will need to be multipurpose to some degree. The ultimate challenge, however, is one-space living, particularly if the space in question is less than generous. All compact multipurpose areas require precise planning and careful execution. It is essential to devote adequate time to assessing your needs. Conduct a thorough review of your possessions and get rid of anything that is surplus to requirements before you begin.

The best solutions for multipurpose areas often rely on fitted elements and built-in features. You may wish to consult an architect or design professional to come up with a scheme or to carry out a custom-build. Any articulated element, such as fold-down bed or pull-out worktop, has to be designed and constructed to a high standard so that it is easy to reconfigure the space on a daily basis.

Work it all out on paper first. Every little bit of space will count. Take accurate measurements and make scale drawings so you can try out different arrangements. Templates of furniture and fittings can help you achieve an optimum layout. If you are going to consult a design professional, these drawings can form the basis of an initial brief.

LEFT: A LONG BUILT-IN WORKTOP, WITH ADDITIONAL SHELVING, PROVIDES A COMPACT AREA FOR A HOME OFFICE WITHIN A MULTIPURPOSE SPACE.

ABOVE: A RECESS PAINTED BLUE DEFINES A SLEEPING AREA. A WORK AREA IS SET UP IN FRONT OF THE WINDOWS TO TAKE ADVANTAGE OF NATURAL LIGHT.

Continued

Multipurpose areas

Points to consider

- Think about grouping areas of activity when it comes to planning the layout. Cooking and eating go naturally together. Sleeping requires more privacy and perhaps a degree of separation or enclosure; the same is true of working areas.
- If the area has high ceilings, think about introducing a mezzanine or platform level.
- Try to arrange the layout to take advantage of natural light. If you work from home during the day, set up a desk or study area near a window to aid concentration.
- Existing servicing arrangements, particularly water and drainage, may dictate where you can site the cooking area and the bathroom. If you have the option, grouping services in a central core can make an efficient use of space. Whatever the case, build in additional flexibility by increasing the number of power points. Make sure that you include an efficient extraction system if the multipurpose space includes a kitchen.
- Successful multipurpose layouts retain a sense of unity while making the distinction between different activities clear. Keep backgrounds plain and try to avoid obstructing sightlines. Lighting, open modular units and semi-partitions are all ways of signalling a shift in function.
- Conceal working areas as far as possible. Articulated, fold-down or pull-out fittings and fixtures allow you to switch from one function to another.

ABOVE: SLIDING SCREENS WITH TRANSLUCENT PANELS SCREEN THE TELEVISION AND OTHER MEDIA EQUIPMENT WHEN NOT IN USE.

RIGHT: THE LAYOUT OF THIS STUDIO IS DEFINED BY THE CENTRAL STAIR LEADING TO THE SLEEPING PLATFORM.

Living rooms

Any living room, no matter how small, must serve one key purpose and that is to provide a place to relax. All too often, however, comfort is undermined by the competing demands of different activities that take place in the same space, or by unnecessary clutter. Think about the functions that your living area currently performs. Could any be shifted elsewhere to create a more peaceful atmosphere?

Enhancing space

- Enlarge existing openings or create new ones. When it comes to generating a feeling of spaciousness, improving the connection between a living area and a garden, terrace or balcony can make a vast difference. Extending the same colour or type of flooring from indoors to out encourages both spaces to be read as a whole.
- Large expanses of mirror, either placed over a fireplace, in an alcove, or positioned to reflect the view from a window, enhance available light and create a sense of openness.
- Never light a living room with a single overhead fitting. Instead, bounce light off walls and ceilings to create a diffused background glow. Shaded floor and table lamps lead the eye from place to place and create overlapping pools of light and shade that are very atmospheric.

ABOVE: BUILT-IN STORAGE KEEPS A MUSIC COLLECTION TIDY AND THE ROOM FREE FROM CLUTTER. IT IS A GOOD IDEA TO SEPARATE FAVOURITES FROM YOUR ARCHIVE TO MAKE RETRIEVAL EASIER.

LEFT: A REAL FIRE PROVIDES A HOSPITABLE FOCUS IN A SMALL LIVING ROOM. THE HEARTH IS A SIMPLE BLACK RECESS WITH NO DETAILING.

Continued

Living rooms

Storage

Aside from bookshelves, which have an intrinsic aesthetic appeal, open storage in a living room generally does not contribute much to the overall mood of relaxation. Instead, plan concealed or fitted storage wherever possible.

- Work with the structure of the room, using alcoves or recesses for fitted cupboards.
- If your storage needs are extensive, devote an entire wall to fitted cupboards. Paint the door fronts to match the rest of the decoration.
- If you are on a tight budget, a collection of matching containers on open shelving is more discreet than leaving CDs, DVDs and the like out on view.

Home media

Most living areas operate as home media centres of some form or another, even in households where there is more than one set. Unlike a fireplace, where people naturally gather, a television screen does not offer the same hospitable focus, especially when it is switched off. Some sort of balance needs to be struck between finding a place to position it where everyone can comfortably watch and preventing it from dominating the room. Flat screens, because they are thin, are easy to conceal behind flush panels. Other media equipment, such as DVD players, are also best concealed or discreetly shelved at low level where they will be least intrusive.

ABOVE: A LARGE INTERNAL OPENING CUT INTO A PARTITION WALL PROVIDES VIEWS THROUGH THE SPACE AND SPREADS NATURAL LIGHT AROUND.

RIGHT: A FLAT SCREEN TV IS POSITIONED ON A LOW BROAD SHELF WHERE IT IS LESS DOMINANT. THERE IS STORAGE SPACE FOR DVDS UNDERNEATH.

Kitchens

A compact kitchen can be supremely efficient and pleasant to use if you plan it properly. There are two routes you can choose: either fit out a separate small area as a highly efficient one-person operation or incorporate a compact kitchen area within a multipurpose living space in order to benefit from a sense of inclusiveness.

Compact layouts

Successful small kitchens tend to be fitted, which makes the most of available space. Except for an arrangement that incorporates a separate island, most of the common types of kitchen layout can be adapted to small spaces.

- In-line layouts, where everything is arranged along one wall, are ideal for kitchens that form part of open-plan spaces. The kitchen can be screened with sliding or folding panels when it is not in use.
- Galley layouts, where units are built into opposite walls, are also efficient and space-saving. You need a minimum of 1.2m (4ft) between the facing units.
- L-shaped layouts and layouts that incorporate a peninsula counter, also work well in multipurpose spaces.
- U-shaped layouts need a little more room, ideally 2m (6½ft) between the arms of the U.
- Most space-saving of all are compact kitchens that are integrated within a single freestanding unit or cabinet.

ABOVE: INTERIOR FITTINGS AND ACCESSORIES MAKE THE MOST OF EVERY LAST BIT OF CUPBOARD SPACE.

LEFT: SLIDING PANELS SCREEN A COMPACT FITTED KITCHEN WHEN IT IS NOT IN USE. THE MATERIALS AND DETAILING ECHO THAT USED THROUGHOUT THE SPACE.

Continued

Kitchens

Points to consider

- Keep preparation areas as clear as possible. Arrange the layout so that tall cupboards are at the end of the worktop.
- Resist the temptation to acquire specialist kitchen gadgets that devour space and are infrequently used. The same is true of kitchen utensils and pots and pans.
- Pull-out worktops can provide more counter space. Other articulated, space-saving features include fold-down tabletops and ironing boards fitted to laundry cupboards.
- Fitted units that are raised up on feet, or where the plinth is omitted, are space-enhancing because they reveal the full extent of the floor.
- Customize drawer and cupboard interiors with dividers, racks and containers to make maximum use of space. Carousel units prevent dead space in corners.
- If you live alone, small-scale appliances may suit your needs very well.
- Choose all-purpose cookware, tableware and glassware. Uniform shapes and sizes stack neatly and are easier to store.
- Seamless detailing reduces visual clutter.
- Materials such as stainless steel and glass reflect light and are space-enhancing.
- Keep in step with what you actually cook and eat to make best use of the space in pantry cupboards. Periodically review basic foodstuffs and discard whatever is past its use-by date.
- If your kitchen is poorly lit, you can borrow natural light from adjacent areas by installing internal portholes or windows.

Eating areas

The separate dining room is becoming increasingly rare these days, which is hardly surprising. Our informal and busy lifestyles mean that it is no longer unthinkable to entertain in the kitchen, as it once was, and the pressure on space in many homes rules out keeping a separate room for occasional use. The natural association of cooking and eating means that many kitchens now serve as eating areas as well. Alternatively, an eating area might occupy part of general living space.

Defining an eating area

In multipurpose spaces, it is important to make some distinction between different activities such as cooking, eating and relaxing. There are various ways in which you can signal a shift of activity to define an eating area.

- Exploit the shape of the space. If your living area is L-shaped, for example, you might set up a table and chairs within the short arm of the L.
- Anchor the eating area within the space: you can position it in front of a window or define it by picking out an adjacent wall in a strong colour or pattern.
- Open room dividers, which do not block light or views, can demarcate different areas within an open-plan space.

ABOVE: A SMALL COUNTER PROVIDES ENOUGH SPACE FOR A SMALL BREAKFAST BAR. PULL-OUT OR FLAP-DOWN ELEMENTS CAN ADD VALUABLE WORK SURFACES.

LEFT: A PAIR OF BENCHES SUSPENDED FROM THE WALLS TRANSFORMS AN ALCOVE INTO AN EATING AREA.

Continued

Eating areas

Furniture

- Fold-down tabletops or pull-out counters can provide enough space for a couple of place settings and make a useful arrangement for light meals and snacks.
- Extendable tables and stackable or folding chairs are a good way of accommodating larger numbers on special occasions.
- If your eating area forms part of a multipurpose space, it can serve other functions between mealtimes, perhaps doing double duty as a working area. Choose a table and chairs that are simple and generic in design to make the shift between one activity and the next more natural.
- Peninsula worktops or half-height dividers that incorporate deep counters can serve as breakfast bars. Similarly, one side of a kitchen island can be used as a place for light meals.
- The sideboard, reinvented as a long, clean-lined low cupboard, is a good place to store table linen, crockery and cutlery.

Lighting

- Light the table with a pendant or a series of pendants hung low enough to avoid glare and high enough to allow unimpeded views across the table. It is essential to shade the light source so you are not dazzled while you eat.
- Where an eating area forms part of a kitchen, put the kitchen lighting on dimmer controls so that you can lower the light levels for dining.

ABOVE: A CHEERFUL COLLECTION OF BAR STOOLS PULLED UP TO A NARROW COUNTER MAKES GOOD USE OF LIMITED FLOOR AREA.

RIGHT: A PAIR OF STOOLS THAT ARE DETAILED AND FINISHED TO MATCH KITCHEN UNITS AND WORKTOP ARE NEAT AND UNOBTRUSIVE.

Bedrooms

Bedrooms principally serve as tranquil retreats from the rest of the household. If your home is on the small side, the chances are that the greater proportion of the space at your disposal will be multipurpose. In that case, the bedroom will inevitably assume an even greater importance as a place of private refuge. As long as your bed is big enough and there is enough room around it for access and changing bed linen, there is no great disadvantage to a small bedroom or sleeping area.

- Clothes storage tends to put the most pressure on bedroom space. Either keep your wardrobe elsewhere, or devote part of the bedroom to fitted clothes storage, which is less intrusive than storage furniture or open clothes rails.
- Avoid central overhead lights, which deaden atmosphere and cause uncomfortable glare when you are in a prone position. Instead, provide background light with sidelights, uplights or table lamps. Adjustable bedside lights are also invaluable for reading in bed. Ideally, bedroom lighting should be dimmable.
- Pay attention to basic orientation when choosing wall colours. Warm up north-facing rooms with cream or warm neutral tones; south-facing rooms can take pure white and shades of blue.

ABOVE: A BED RAISED UP ON A PLATFORM EXPLOITS THE ADDITIONAL HEIGHT PROVIDED BY A HIGH CEILING.

LEFT: SMALL BEDROOMS CAN BE APPEALINGLY COSY. HERE, FULL USE IS MADE OF THE UNDER-BED AREA FOR FITTED CUPBOARDS AND DRAWERS.

Continued

Bedrooms

Open-plan bedrooms

- Sleeping platforms can represent an efficient use of the space in a room with a relatively high ceiling. You can either construct a platform or build a mezzanine level accessed by stairs. A high-level bed does not require full head height, simply enough room for you to sit up in bed without banging your head. This type of arrangement also provides the opportunity to build in storage space underneath or create a work or study area. Safe and secure access will be required and some form of guardrail or protective barrier is also a sensible idea.

- Taking the en suite arrangement to its logical conclusion, you can minimally separate a bedroom from a bathroom by partitioning the two areas with a half-height screen that serves as an over-scaled headboard on the sleeping side of the space.

- Sleeping pods are another form of minimal enclosure for a sleeping area located within an open-plan space. By surrounding a bed with some form of screening, such as slatted blinds or translucent panels, you can create a contemporary update on the traditional four-poster arrangement.

ABOVE: A SLEEPING AREA TUCKED UNDER THE EAVES IN A CONVERTED ROOF SPACE IS LIT BY TWO SKYLIGHTS AND MINIMALLY SCREENED FROM THE LEVEL BELOW.

RIGHT: A CONTEMPORARY FOLD-DOWN WALL BED IS ONE OPTION WHERE SPACE IS TIGHT. MODERN DESIGNS ARE WELL ENGINEERED AND COMFORTABLE.

Bathrooms

Like small kitchens, small bathrooms are often best treated as fitted spaces, with the necessary fixtures integrated within a built-in framework of some kind. Another option is to turn the space into a wet room, where the shower drains directly into the floor. Bathroom suppliers and major retailers offer in-house design services to help you make the most of the layout.

- Only include essential fixtures. A bidet may well be an optional extra and you could do without a bathtub if you prefer taking showers to baths.
- Investigate whether you can directly increase the floor area, by moving a partition forwards, for example.
- Consider replacing a door that opens inwards with a sliding panel. Bifold or sliding shower screens also save space.
- Underfloor heating is a good space-saving option; alternatively opt for a slimline wall-hung radiator or heated towel rail.
- Keep decoration simple and coordinate colours and materials.
- Build in storage wherever possible: under sinks, between sinks and toilets, or at either end of the bath.
- Top lighting in the form of skylights or rooflights enhances the sense of volume and can counteract a feeling of enclosure.
- Recessed downlights around the perimeter of the room increase apparent breadth.
- A bathtub, sink or toilet can be positioned under a sloping ceiling provided there is enough head height at the front for access.

ABOVE: A BATHTUB IS TUCKED UNDER A SLOPING CEILING TO MAKE THE MOST OF AVAILABLE SPACE.

LEFT: A WALK-IN SHOWER IS SCREENED BY A FRAMELESS GLASS ENCLOSURE. RECESSED CUBBYHOLES PROVIDE STORAGE FOR BATH LINEN.

Continued

Bathrooms

Fittings & fixtures

Take the time to research the market and visit bathroom showrooms. Try out fixtures by standing at them, sitting on them or lying in them to assess whether they are right for your height and frame.

- Many manufacturers produce compact ranges of fittings and fixtures for small bathrooms.
- Shaped, angled or corner fittings can be space-saving. A tapered bathtub, for example, can be positioned across the width of a space rather than down its length, which can make a layout more workable.
- Wall-hung sinks and toilets, which keep the floor area clear, are more space-enhancing than pedestal versions. Make sure the wall can bear the weight. The dummy panel that conceals the cistern of a wall-hung toilet can provide an opportunity for built-in storage.

Wet rooms

- The floor should be laid expertly so that water runs readily into the drain.
- Flooring materials should be non-slip.
- The underlying wall and floor structure generally requires additional waterproofing, which can be achieved by applying a bituminous layer or polythene membrane ('tanking') or lining in marine ply.
- Surface cladding needs to be as waterproof as possible. Mosaic, ceramic or stone tiles are all suitable materials.

ABOVE: HERE, A HEATED TOWEL RAIL IS FITTED TO EXPLOIT AVAILABLE WALL SPACE; SMALL BATHROOMS CALL FOR CAREFUL PLANNING.

RIGHT: A TALL GLASS SCREEN AND LARGE MIRROR REFLECT LIGHT TO ENHANCE THE SENSE OF SPACE IN A SMALL SHOWER ROOM.

Dressing rooms

Clothes storage puts pressure on space in small bedrooms. If you have no option but to keep your wardrobe in your bedroom, it is best to adopt a fitted approach. Freestanding wardrobes and chests of drawers can be very intrusive in a room that already includes a large piece of furniture, and open rails expose clothes to fading, dust and moths. Look for ways to create compact built-in closets or dressing rooms elsewhere in the home, preferably near the bedroom or bathroom, where dressing and undressing takes place. If they are wide enough, adjacent hallways, short corridors or vestibules can be lined with fitted cupboards and shelves.

Before you begin to plan fitted clothes storage, undertake a serious review of what you own. It is estimated that most people only wear about 20 per cent of their wardrobe on a regular basis, which means that 80 per cent of the space given over to clothes storage is wasted. Get rid of clothing that does not fit you, that does not suit you, that you have not worn for a long time or that requires expensive repair. Rotating clothes on a seasonal basis can also ease pressure on space and provides a natural time for this type of critical review.

ABOVE: A DRESSING ROOM IS SCREENED FROM THE ADJACENT AREA BY A SLIDING TRANSLUCENT PANEL.

LEFT: MOBILE STORAGE UNITS ON CASTORS, IN COMBINATION WITH A OPEN HANGING RAIL, MAKES A HANDSOME ARRANGEMENT FOR CLOTHES STORAGE.

Continued

Dressing rooms

Points to consider

- Sources of fitted clothes storage include major retailers who produce affordable ranges of fitted wardrobe units, and storage or closet system specialists, whose ranges tend to be more up-market. Alternatively, you can commission a builder or carpenter to fit out the space to your specification.
- You will need a combination of hanging space – double-hung if possible – and drawers or shelves for items best stored flat.
- Hanging storage requires a depth of at least 60cm (24in).
- Drawers need a clearance of 1m (3ft) in front.
- Sliding, bifolding or concertina doors are space-saving. You can also screen fitted storage with blinds.
- Customize the interior of fitted wardrobes with shoe tidies, drawer dividers, lidded boxes and containers, and racks and rails for storing small items or organizing accessories. Make use of the back of closet doors.
- A full-length mirror is essential. Mirrored closet doors are ideal; otherwise you can attach a mirror to the back of a full-height door or panel.
- Make use of the space underneath the bed to store bulky jumpers and the like. Some beds incorporate drawers or compartments in their bases. Flat-lidded plastic containers on wheels keep moths out and are ideal for storing shoes under the bed.
- Decorate doors and drawer fronts to match the walls or opt for translucent panels, which are self-effacing.

ABOVE: A WALL DEVOTED TO FITTED STORAGE IN A BEDROOM PROVIDES PLENTY OF SPACE FOR CLOTHES AS WELL AS A PLACE TO CONCEAL A TELEVISION.

RIGHT: CUSTOM-DESIGNED SHOE STORAGE TAKES THE FORM OF A SLIDING BOX-LIKE CONSTRUCTION THAT ALSO SERVES AS A PARTITION FOR THE BATHROOM.

Children's rooms

Nothing brings spatial limitations into sharper focus than children, which is why moving house so often coincides with the arrival of a new baby. Failing a move, the onset of family life provides a good opportunity to rethink the way you use your home as a whole.

Re-allocating space

It makes sense, especially if your second child is on the way, to juggle sleeping arrangements so that the biggest bedroom is the children's room. When children are pre-school age and for some time after, play is largely floor-based and if they do not have enough room in their bedroom, you might find yourself sharing a living room or kitchen with a train set or Lego model. Later, when each child requires a room of his or her own, you can consider dividing up the space in some other way.

Space-saving beds

- When children are sharing a room, bunk beds are a popular option as they maximize floor area. Do not allow a child under five or six to sleep on the top. Ensure the design conforms to safety standards: guardrails are mandatory, as are secure ladders.
- Some modular designs combine high-level beds with storage or study areas underneath.

ABOVE: A LONG LOW BOOKCASE AT THE BASE OF A BED HOUSES A COLLECTION OF PICTURE BOOKS FOR BEDTIME READING.

LEFT: LOW-LEVEL CUPBOARDS ALLOW CHILDREN TO ACCESS THEIR TOYS AND BELONGINGS EASILY. SHELVING MAKES GOOD ALL-PURPOSE STORAGE AT ANY AGE.

Continued

Children's rooms

ABOVE: BUNK BEDS ARE POPULAR OPTIONS WHERE CHILDREN SHARE A ROOM. HERE, THE LOWER BUNK DOUBLES UP AS AN ADDITIONAL PLACE TO SIT.

RIGHT: A CUSTOM-BUILT ARRANGEMENT OF BUNK BEDS, TUCKED INTO A RECESS, FEATURES NARROW SHELVING AT EACH LEVEL FOR STORING FAVOURITE TOYS AND PICTURE BOOKS.

Storage

- Keep ahead of the game by reviewing toys, possessions and clothing on a regular basis, discarding what is outgrown in either a physical or developmental sense. Give your child a say in the process so you do not unwittingly dispose of a well-loved item before he or she is ready to let it go.

- Containers of various descriptions, from plastic stacking boxes to cloth bags, are indispensable for children's storage. You can use colour-coded containers to sort and store one child's possessions from another's or to organize multi-piece games and puzzles. Modular, stackable designs are space-saving, as are flat containers on castors that can be wheeled under the bed.

- Resist the temptation to fit out a young child's room with miniature items of storage furniture; these will be quickly outgrown.

- When children are small, low-level pegs and rails keep belongings accessible.

- Built-in shelving makes good all-purpose storage from the pre-school years right up to adolescence.

- Ensure that all tall pieces of freestanding storage furniture, such as bookcases, are securely anchored to the wall to prevent them from toppling or being pulled over.

- Make room for display. Children like to see their favourite possessions out on view. In the early years, out of sight means out of mind, so a seamless fitted approach is more or less ruled out until children are older.

Working areas

Working from home, some or all of the time, places its own demands on a space. Much will depend on the nature of the work in question. If you only have yourself to worry about, and your work is largely computer-based, a home office can be slotted into a number of different areas relatively easily. For larger scale operations, particularly if you employ staff, you may need to consider converting an attic or basement for the purpose or make use of an outbuilding or shed.

Siting a work station

- All working areas need some form of separation from the rest of the household to aid concentration. Ideally, you should also be able to leave work in progress without having to clear everything away at the end of the day.
- Views help to focus the mind. A built-in workstation or desk positioned in front of or alongside a window is good for creative daydreaming. A good quality of natural light is also an advantage, even if it comes from an overhead skylight.
- Home offices can be set up on generously sized landings.
- The space under the stairs can be fitted out as a compact working area.
- Workstations built into a wall of storage, which can be screened off when not in use, are most discreet. Some integrated work areas incorporate pull-out surfaces to serve as a desktop.
- Consider siting your desk away from an area in the home where you can easily get distracted or drawn into a conversation.

ABOVE: THIS WORKING AREA OCCUPIES PART OF A CONVERTED ATTIC AND IS LIT BY A SKYLIGHT SET INTO THE PLANE OF THE ROOF.

LEFT: AN EXCEPTIONALLY DISCREET HOME OFFICE IS SCREENED BY A TAMBOUR SHUTTER WHEN NOT IN USE.

Continued

Working areas

Points to consider

- For sedentary or desk-bound work it is essential to equip yourself with an ergonomic task chair designed specifically to prevent back pain. An ordinary kitchen chair will not provide adequate support or permit the changes of posture and position that are necessary if you are going to be sitting in one place for a matter of hours.
- Wireless technology means that you do not necessarily have to provide space near your desk for ancillary home office devices such as printers and scanners.
- Concentrated work on paper requires a much higher level of light than is comfortable in a general living area – up to four times as much. Working on the computer requires slightly less because the screen is lit. Uplighters provide good background light for working on screen. Supplement with angled task lights for reading documents or highlighting the keyboard.
- Think about storage. Only keep what relates to the task at hand on the desktop. You should arrange shelving or some form of storage for reference materials, back-up supplies and recent projects in close proximity. Your archive, along with accounts and tax returns, can be kept at further remove in deep storage. Do not forget to back up your work electronically on a regular basis.

ABOVE: A SMALL HOME OFFICE BENEFITS FROM THE NATURAL LIGHT PROVIDED BY A GLAZED WALL. FRESH AIR AND ACCESS TO THE GARDEN ARE A BONUS.

RIGHT: A NARROW WORKSURFACE RUNS ALONG THE LENGTH OF A MEZZANINE LEVEL. GOOD TASKING LIGHTING IS ESSENTIAL.

Index

Acknowledgements

The publisher would like to thank Red Cover Picture Library for their kind permission to reproduce the following photographs

2 Paul Ryan-Goff; 6–7 Andrew Boyd; 10 Henry Wilson; 11 Mike Daines; 12 Jennifer Cawley; 13 Henry Wilson; 16 Jake Fitzjones; 17 Dan Duchars (Neil Lerner Kitchens); 18 Paul Massey; 19 Johnny Bouchier; 21 Jake Fitzjones; 23 Winfried Heinze; 24 Steve Dalton; 25 Alun Callender; 26 Graham Atkins-Hughes; 27 Trine Thorsen (Designer Nicki Buttenschon, Stylist: Alessandro D'Orazio & Jannicke K. Eriksen; 28 Trine Thorsen; 29 Winfried Heinze; 30 Andrew Wood; 31 Chris Tubbs; 32 Winfried Heinze; 33 Andrew Wood; 34 Guglielmo Galvin; 35 Andrew Twort; 36 Winfried Heinze; 37 Michael Freeman; 38 Grant Scott; 39 Andrew Boyd; 40 Niall McDiarmid; 41 Henry Wilson; 42 Dan Duchars; 43 James Balston; 44 Debi Treloar; 45 Andrew Wood; 46 Tom Scott; 47 Jake Fitzjones (Architect Neville Morgan); 51 Nick Carter; 52 Michael Freeman; 53 Ed Reeve; 55 Jennifer Cawley; 56 Graham Atkins-Hughes (Architect: Sally Vogel); 57 Huntley Hedworth; 58 Jake Fitzjones (Architect: Neville Morgan; 59 Ed Reeve (Designer: Monica Mauti Equihua); 60 Holly Jolliffe; 61 Graham Atkins-Hughes; 62 Paul Massey; 63 Home Journal/Red Cover; 64 Paul Massey; 65 Henry Wilson; 66 Graham Atkins-Hughes; 68 Huntley Hedworth; 70 Jake Fitzjones (Architect: Neville Morgan); 71 Mike Daines (Designer: Jo Warman); 74 Johnny Bouchier; 75 Winfried Heinze; 76 Jake Fitzjones; 77 Henry Wilson; 78 Alun Callender; 80 James Balston (Architect: MPS); 81 Warren Smith (Architect: Honky, Designer: Honky Design); 82 Tria Giovan; 83 Jake Fitzjones (Neil Lerner Kitchens); 84 Graham Atkins-Hughes; 85 Graham Atkins-Hughes; 86 Paul Ryan-Goff; 87 Allun Callender; 88 Lucinda Symons; 89 Ed Reeve (Storage designer: Jona Warbey); 90 Douglas Gibb; 91 James Merrell; 92 Winfried Heinze; 93 Ed Reeve; 94 David Hiscock; 95 Winfried Heinze; 96 Winfried Heinze; 97 Jake Fitzjones (Architect: Paul Archer); 98 Jake Fitzjones; 99 Patrick Spence; 100 Chris Tubbs; 101 Andrew Twort; 102 Trine Thorsen; 103 Tria Giovan; 104 Lucinda Symons; 105 Winfried Heinze (Interior Designer: Lisa Weeks at W Design International, Furniture Designer: Amy Somerville at Somerville Scott & Co); 106 Jake Fitzjones (Architect: Neil Lerner Kitchens); 107 Michael Freeman; 108 Christopher Drake (Designer: Annie Stevens); 109 Winfried Heinze.

Except for the following photographs: 20 Thomas Stewart/Conran Octopus; 22 Chris Tubbs/Conran Octopus; 50 Chris Tubbs/Conran Octopus; 54 Chris Tubbs/Conran Octopus; 67 Chris Tubbs/Conran Octopus; 69 Thomas Stewart/Conran Octopus; 79 Chris Tubbs/Conran Octopus.

First published in 2010 by Conran Octopus Ltd, a part of Octopus Publishing Group, Endeavour House, 189 Shaftesbury Avenue, London WC2H 8JG www.octopusbooks.co.uk

A Hachette UK Company www.hachette.co.uk

Distributed in the United States and Canada by Octopus Books USA, c/o Hachette Book Group USA, 237 Park Avenue, New York, NY 10017 USA

Text copyright © Conran Octopus Ltd 2010 Design and layout copyright © Conran Octopus Ltd 2010

British Library Cataloguing-in-Publication Data. A catalogue record for this book is available from the British Library.

Consultant Editor: Elizabeth Wilhide

Publisher: Lorraine Dickey
Managing Editor: Sybella Marlow
Editor: Bridget Hopkinson

Art Director: Jonathan Christie
Picture Researcher: Liz Boyd
Design Assistant: Mayumi Hashimoto

Production: Caroline Alberti

ISBN: 978 1 84091 552 5
Printed in China